Hearty Stews

Table of Contents

Lamb and Vegetable Stew

2 cups sliced mushrooms
1 large red bell pepper, diced
1 large carrot, cut into $\frac{1}{2}$-inch slices
1 small unpeeled new potato, diced
1 small parsnip, cut into $\frac{1}{2}$-inch slices
1 large leek, white part only, chopped
1 clove garlic, minced
$\frac{1}{2}$ cup reduced-sodium chicken broth
$\frac{1}{2}$ teaspoon dried thyme
$\frac{1}{4}$ teaspoon dried rosemary
$\frac{1}{8}$ teaspoon black pepper
12 ounces lamb shoulder meat, cut into 1-inch pieces
2 tablespoons all-purpose flour
$\frac{1}{2}$ teaspoon salt

Slow Cooker Directions

1. Place mushrooms, bell pepper, carrot, potato, parsnip, leek and garlic in slow cooker. Stir in broth, thyme, rosemary and black pepper. Add lamb. Cover; cook on LOW 6 to 7 hours.

2. Combine flour and 2 tablespoons liquid from slow cooker in small bowl. Stir flour mixture into slow cooker. Cover; cook 10 minutes. Stir in salt. *Makes 4 servings*

Hearty Beef Barley Stew

2 cups baby carrots
1 package (10 ounces) fresh mushrooms, sliced
1½ pounds boneless beef chuck steak, cut into 1-inch cubes
1 envelope LIPTON® RECIPE SECRETS® Onion Soup Mix
2 cans (14½ ounces each) beef broth
1 can (14½ ounces) diced tomatoes, undrained
2 cups water
¾ cup uncooked pearled barley
1 cup frozen green peas
Salt and ground black pepper, to taste

1. In slow cooker, layer carrots, mushrooms and beef. Combine soup mix, broth, tomatoes, water and barley; pour over beef.

2. Cook, covered, on low 8 to 10 hours or on high 4 to 6 hours, or until beef is tender.

3. Stir in peas and cook, covered, 5 minutes, or until heated through. Season, if desired, with salt and ground black pepper.

Makes 8 servings

Prep Time: 10 minutes
Cook Time: 4 hours, 5 minutes (high)

California Fish Stew

3 cups Zinfandel or other dry red wine, divided
1 quart mussels (in shells), cleaned*
¼ cup olive oil
1 package (8 ounces) mushrooms, sliced
1 green bell pepper, chopped
1 onion, chopped
2 cloves garlic, minced
1 can (28 ounces) whole Italian plum tomatoes, undrained
¼ cup tomato paste
1 teaspoon salt
½ teaspoon black pepper
3 pounds striped bass or other firm fish fillets, cut into bite-size pieces
2 tablespoons finely chopped fresh basil
1 pound crabmeat, picked over to remove any shell
1 pound medium raw shrimp, peeled
3 tablespoons chopped fresh Italian parsley

Discard mussels that stay open when tapped with your fingers. To clean mussels, scrub with stiff brush under cold running water. To debeard, pull threads from shells with fingers.

1. Bring 1 cup wine to a boil in Dutch oven. Add mussels; cover and reduce heat to low. Steam 5 to 7 minutes or until shells open. Transfer to large bowl with slotted spoon. (Discard any unopened shells.) Strain cooking liquid through cheesecloth; set aside.

2. Heat oil in Dutch oven over medium heat. Add mushrooms, bell pepper, onion and garlic; cook and stir 3 minutes. Add tomatoes; cook 4 minutes. Stir in reserved cooking liquid, tomato paste and remaining 2 cups wine. Add salt and black pepper; simmer 20 minutes.

3. Add fish and basil; cook 5 minutes or until fish begins to flake when tested with fork. Add mussels, crabmeat and shrimp. Cook 3 minutes or until shrimp turn pink and opaque, stirring occasionally. Sprinkle with parsley; serve immediately. *Makes 10 to 12 servings*

Asian Beef Stew

1½ **pounds boneless beef round steak, thinly sliced**
2 **onions, cut into ¼-inch slices**
2 **stalks celery, sliced**
2 **carrots, sliced *or* 1 cup baby carrots**
1 **cup sliced mushrooms**
1 **cup orange juice**
1 **cup beef broth**
⅓ **cup hoisin sauce**
2 **tablespoons cornstarch**
1 **to 2 teaspoons Chinese five-spice powder or curry powder**
1 **cup frozen peas, thawed**
  Hot cooked rice
  Chopped fresh cilantro (optional)

Slow Cooker Directions

1. Layer beef, onions, celery, carrots and mushrooms in slow cooker.

2. Blend orange juice, broth, hoisin sauce, cornstarch and five-spice powder in small bowl. Pour into slow cooker. Cover; cook on LOW 6 to 8 hours or on HIGH 5 hours or until beef is tender.

3. Stir in peas. Cook 20 minutes or until peas are tender. Serve with rice. Garnish with cilantro. *Makes 6 servings*

Italian Stew Bread Bowls

4 round sourdough loaves (8 ounces each)
¼ cup (½ stick) butter, melted
2 tablespoons olive oil, divided
1 cup chopped onion
1 medium green bell pepper, chopped
8 ounces eggplant, cut into ½-inch cubes
4 ounces whole mushrooms, quartered
1 can (about 14 ounces) stewed tomatoes
1 cup water
2 tablespoons tomato paste
1 teaspoon dried oregano
¼ teaspoon dried rosemary
⅛ teaspoon red pepper flakes
1 can (about 15 ounces) kidney beans, rinsed and drained
¾ teaspoon salt
¼ cup chopped fresh basil
4 slices provolone cheese, cut into thin strips

1. Preheat oven to 350°F. Cut ½-inch lid off bread loaves. Remove bread from interior, leaving ½-inch-thick bowl. (Reserve extra bread for another use.) Brush inside of bowls and lids with melted butter. Place directly on oven rack, buttered side up. Bake about 15 minutes or until crisp. Set aside.

2. Heat 1 tablespoon oil in Dutch oven over medium-high heat. Add onion and bell pepper; cook and stir 4 minutes or until onion is translucent. Add eggplant, mushrooms, tomatoes, water, tomato paste, oregano, rosemary and pepper flakes. Bring to a boil. Reduce heat; cover and simmer 25 minutes. Add beans and salt. Cook, uncovered, 15 minutes or until thickened slightly. Remove from heat; stir in basil and remaining 1 tablespoon oil.

3. Place 1 bread bowl on each plate. Ladle soup into bread bowls. Top each with 1 slice cheese. Let stand 2 minutes to allow cheese to melt slightly before serving. *Makes 4 servings*

Jerk Turkey Stew

1 tablespoon vegetable oil
1 small red onion, chopped
1 clove garlic, minced
½ teaspoon ground ginger
¼ teaspoon salt
¼ teaspoon black pepper
⅛ to ¼ teaspoon ground red pepper*
⅛ teaspoon ground allspice
1 can (28 ounces) diced tomatoes
3 cups diced cooked turkey
2 cups diced cooked sweet potatoes (½-inch pieces)
½ cup turkey broth or gravy
1 tablespoon lime juice
1 tablespoon minced fresh chives

Use ⅛ teaspoon for a mildly hot dish; use ¼ teaspoon for a very hot dish.

1. Heat oil in Dutch oven over medium heat. Add onion and garlic; cook and stir 5 minutes. Add ginger, salt, black pepper, red pepper and allspice; cook 20 seconds. Stir in tomatoes, turkey, sweet potatoes and broth. Reduce heat to low; simmer 15 minutes.

2. Stir in lime juice; cover and let stand 10 minutes. Sprinkle with chives just before serving.   *Makes 4 servings*

Tip: Instead of sweet potatoes, add diced cooked white potatoes or simply serve this stew over cooked rice.

Curried Chicken & Winter Vegetable Stew

1 pound boneless skinless chicken breasts, cut into ½-inch cubes
1 tablespoon curry powder
3½ cups reduced-sodium chicken broth
1 can (about 14 ounces) diced tomatoes
2 medium turnips, cut into 1-inch pieces
2 medium carrots, halved lengthwise, then cut crosswise into 1-inch slices
1 medium onion, chopped
½ cup raisins (optional)
¼ cup tomato paste

1. Spray large saucepan with nonstick cooking spray; heat over medium heat. Add chicken; cook 5 minutes or until lightly browned, stirring occasionally. Add curry powder; cook and stir 1 minute.

2. Stir in broth, tomatoes, turnips, carrots, onion, raisins, if desired, and tomato paste. Bring to a boil. Reduce heat to low; cover and simmer 15 minutes or until vegetables are tender, stirring occasionally.

Makes 6 servings

Serving Suggestion: Serve with couscous or brown rice.

Beef Stew in Red Wine

1½ pounds beef round steak, cut into 1-inch cubes
1½ cups dry red wine
2 teaspoons olive oil
Peel of ½ orange
2 cloves garlic, thinly sliced
1 bay leaf
½ teaspoon dried thyme
⅛ teaspoon black pepper
8 ounces mushrooms, quartered
8 sun-dried tomatoes, quartered
1 can (about 14 ounces) reduced-sodium beef broth
6 unpeeled small red or new potatoes, cut into wedges
1 cup baby carrots
1 cup fresh pearl onions, outer skins removed
1 tablespoon cornstarch mixed with 2 tablespoons water

1. Combine beef, wine, oil, orange peel, garlic, bay leaf, thyme and pepper in large bowl. Cover and refrigerate at least 2 hours or overnight.

2. Place beef mixture, mushrooms and tomatoes in Dutch oven. Add enough broth to just cover ingredients. Bring to a boil over high heat. Reduce heat to low; cover and simmer 1 hour.

3. Add potatoes, carrots and onions; cover and cook 20 to 25 minutes or until vegetables are tender. Remove meat and vegetables with slotted spoon; cover and set aside. Discard orange peel and bay leaf.

4. Stir cornstarch mixture into sauce in Dutch oven. Increase heat to medium; cook and stir until sauce is slightly thickened. Return meat and vegetables to sauce; heat through. *Makes 6 servings*

Fiesta Chicken Stew with Cornbread Dumplings

    6 boneless, skinless chicken thighs, cut in 1-inch pieces
    1/4 cup all-purpose flour
    1/2 teaspoon salt
    1/2 teaspoon cumin
    2 tablespoons vegetable oil, divided
    1 medium sweet potato, peeled, cut in 1-inch chunks
    1 medium onion, chopped
    1 large clove garlic, minced
    2 cans (14 1/2 ounces each) fat-free, reduced-sodium chicken broth
 1 1/2 cups prepared medium-hot chunky salsa
    1/2 teaspoon oregano
    1 medium zucchini, cut in 1-inch chunks
 1 1/2 cups frozen whole kernel corn
    1/4 teaspoon hot pepper sauce
        Cornbread Dumplings (recipe follows)

In plastic bag, place flour, salt and cumin; shake to mix. Add chicken, one third at a time, shaking to coat. In Dutch oven, place 1 tablespoon vegetable oil and heat to medium-high temperature. Add chicken and cook, stirring, about 10 minutes or until chicken is brown. Remove chicken to bowl; set aside. To same pan, add remaining 1 tablespoon oil and heat to medium-high temperature. Add sweet potato, onion and garlic. Cook, stirring, about 5 minutes or until onion is soft. Return chicken to pan; add broth, salsa and oregano. Heat to boiling; cover, reduce heat to low and cook 10 minutes. Add zucchini, corn and hot pepper sauce; heat to boiling. Drop Cornbread Dumplings on top of boiling stew; reduce heat to medium-low and cook, covered, 10 minutes. Remove cover and simmer 5 minutes or until dumplings are cooked through and chicken and vegetables are fork tender.

Makes 6 servings

Cornbread Dumplings: In bowl, place 1 package (6 1/2 to 8 ounces) corn muffin mix. Stir in 1/2 teaspoon cumin. Add 1 beaten egg, 2 tablespoons melted margarine and 3 tablespoons low-fat milk; stir to form a thick batter. Cook as directed above.

Favorite recipe from **Delmarva Poultry Industry, Inc.**

Turkey and White Bean Stew

1 tablespoon olive oil
1 cup chopped onion
½ cup sliced celery
3 large cloves garlic, finely chopped
2 cans (15 ounces each) cannellini or other white beans, rinsed
    and drained, divided
1½ cups water
2 tablespoons dry white wine (optional)
1 teaspoon MAGGI® Granulated Chicken Flavor Bouillon
2 cups shredded cooked turkey
⅔ cup NESTLÉ® CARNATION® Evaporated Lowfat 2% Milk
1 tablespoon chopped parsley

HEAT oil in large saucepan over medium-high heat. Add onion and celery; cook for 3 to 5 minutes or until just tender. Stir in garlic; cook for 30 seconds.

ADD *half* of beans to saucepan; mash with fork. Stir in *remaining* beans, water, wine and bouillon. Bring to a boil; reduce heat and cook for 5 minutes. Stir in turkey and evaporated milk. Cook for 3 minutes or until heated through. Stir in parsley. Season with ground black pepper.

Makes 4 servings

Prep Time: 10 minutes
Cooking Time: 15 minutes

Brunswick Stew

1 whole chicken (about 4 pounds), cut up
2 quarts water
1 stalk celery (including leaves), cut into 2-inch pieces
1 onion, quartered
1 clove garlic, halved
2 teaspoons salt
1 teaspoon whole black peppercorns
1 can (about 14 ounces) diced tomatoes
2 russet potatoes, peeled and cubed
1 onion, thinly sliced
¼ cup tomato paste
1 teaspoon sugar
½ teaspoon dried thyme
½ teaspoon ground black pepper
⅛ teaspoon garlic powder
   Dash hot pepper sauce
1 package (10 ounces) frozen lima beans
1 package (10 ounces) frozen corn

1. Place chicken and water in Dutch oven; bring to a boil over medium-high heat. Skim off foam. Add celery, quartered onion, garlic, salt and peppercorns; return to a boil. Reduce heat to medium-low; cover and simmer 2½ to 3 hours or until chicken is cooked through (165°F).

2. Remove chicken from broth; cool slightly. Remove meat, discarding skin and bones. Cut enough chicken into 1-inch pieces to measure 3 cups. (Reserve remaining chicken for another use.)

3. Strain and reserve broth through double thickness of cheesecloth. Discard vegetables; skim off fat. Return 1 quart broth to Dutch oven. (Reserve remaining broth for another use.)

4. Add tomatoes, potatoes, sliced onion, tomato paste, sugar, thyme, ground black pepper, garlic powder and hot pepper sauce. Bring to a boil over medium-high heat. Reduce heat to medium-low; cover and simmer 30 minutes. Add beans and corn; cover and simmer 5 minutes. Add chicken; cook 5 minutes or until heated through.

Makes 6 to 8 servings

Pork and Anaheim Stew

 2 tablespoons olive oil, divided
1½ pounds boneless pork shoulder, trimmed of fat and cut into
  ½-inch pieces
 6 Anaheim peppers,* split in half lengthwise, seeded and sliced
 4 cloves garlic, minced
 1 pound tomatillos, papery skins removed, rinsed and chopped
 2 cups chopped onions
 1 can (about 15 ounces) yellow hominy, rinsed and drained
 1 can (about 14 ounces) chicken broth
 2 teaspoons chili powder
1½ teaspoons sugar
 1 teaspoon ground cumin
 1 teaspoon dried oregano
 1 teaspoon liquid smoke
 ½ teaspoon salt

Anaheim peppers can sting and irritate the skin, so wear rubber gloves when handling peppers and do not touch your eyes.

Slow Cooker Directions

1. Heat 1 tablespoon oil in large skillet over medium-high heat. Brown pork in batches. Transfer to slow cooker.

2. Add Anaheim peppers to same skillet; cook and stir 5 minutes or until edges are very brown. Add garlic; cook and stir 30 seconds. Transfer to slow cooker.

3. Stir in tomatillos, onions, hominy, broth, chili powder, sugar, cumin and oregano. Cover; cook on LOW 10 hours or on HIGH 5 hours.

4. Stir in remaining 1 tablespoon oil, liquid smoke and salt.

Makes 4 to 6 servings

Prep Time: 30 minutes
Cook Time: 10 hours (LOW) or 5 hours (HIGH)

Beef Stew with a Coffee Kick

⅓ cup all-purpose flour
1 teaspoon salt
½ teaspoon garlic powder
½ teaspoon dried marjoram
½ teaspoon black pepper
3 tablespoons vegetable oil
2 pounds beef stew meat, cut into 1½-inch cubes
1 can (about 14 ounces) diced tomatoes
1¼ cups strong brewed coffee, at room temperature
2 teaspoons beef bouillon granules
2 cups cubed peeled potatoes
4 stalks celery, cut into ½-inch pieces
4 medium carrots, cut into ½-inch slices
3 small onions, quartered
1 bay leaf

1. Preheat oven to 325°F. Whisk flour, salt, garlic powder, marjoram and pepper in small bowl.

2. Heat oil in Dutch oven over medium-high heat. Brown meat on all sides in batches. Sprinkle flour mixture over meat; cook and stir about 2 minutes or until flour is slightly browned. Stir in tomatoes, coffee and bouillon granules, mixing well and scraping up browned bits on bottom of Dutch oven. Bring to a simmer. Stir in potatoes, celery, carrots, onions and bay leaf.

3. Cover and bake 2½ to 3 hours or until meat is tender, stirring every hour. Remove bay leaf before serving.   *Makes 6 servings*

Tip: For a thinner stew, add additional ½ to ¾ cup coffee 15 minutes before serving.

Pepper & Pineapple Pork Stew

- **4 top loin pork chops, cut into 1-inch cubes**
- **4 carrots, sliced**
- **½ cup chicken broth**
- **3 tablespoons teriyaki sauce**
- **1 tablespoon cornstarch**
- **1 (8-ounce) can pineapple chunks in juice, drained and juice reserved**
- **1 green bell pepper, seeded and cut into 1-inch pieces**

Slow Cooker Directions

Brown pork cubes in hot skillet, if desired. Mix pork, carrots, broth and teriyaki sauce in 3½-quart slow cooker; cover and cook on low for 7 to 8 hours. Mix cornstarch with reserved pineapple juice; stir into pork mixture. Stir in pineapple and green pepper. Cover and cook on high 15 minutes or until thickened and bubbly.   *Makes 4 servings*

Favorite recipe from **National Pork Board**

Acknowledgments

The publisher would like to thank the companies and organizations listed below for the use of their recipes and photographs in this publication.

Delmarva Poultry Industry, Inc.

National Pork Board

Nestlé USA

Unilever